IMA ON THE BIMA

MY MOMMY IS A RABBI

Written by
MINDY AVRA PORTNOY

Illustrated by
STEFFI KAREN RUBIN

KAR-BEN COPIES, INC.   ROCKVILLE, MD

To Ceala Eloise and Barney Samuel

Library of Congress Cataloging-in-Publication Data

Portnoy, Mindy Avra.
  Ima on the bima.

  Summary: Through the eyes of her daughter, describes
the activities of Mindy Avra Portnoy in her job as a
rabbi.
  1. Rabbis—Office—Juvenile literature. 2. Portnoy,
Mindy Avra—Juvenile literature. [1. Rabbis.
1. Portnoy, Mindy Avra. 3. Occupation] I. Rubin,
Steffi, ill. II. Title.
BM652.P65 1986   296.8'34 [B]   86-3023
ISBN 0-930494-55-5
ISBN 0-930494-54-7 (pbk.)

Published by KAR-BEN COPIES, INC., Rockville, MD
Printed in the United States of America

I call my mommy Ima. That means Mommy in Hebrew. Other people call her Rabbi. That is her job.

Ima wears a little hat called a kippah. It has lots of pretty colors. I have a kippah, too. It has my name on it, so if I lose it, someone can find it and bring it back to me.

At services and weddings, Ima wears a special shawl called a tallit. She says a blessing before she puts it on.

Ima has an office in the synagogue. She goes there everyday. Sometimes I go, too. Everywhere I look there are books and books and books. Some are in Hebrew, others are in English. Ima keeps a shelf of books and toys just for me.

Many people visit Ima in her office. Yesterday a very tall man with a moustache came. He looked sad. When the man came out of Ima's office, I smiled at him. He smiled back at me. Part of Ima's job is to make people happier, and I try to help Ima do her job.

Happy people visit Ima, too. Some of them are getting married. Ima performs the weddings. She stands with the bride and groom under the chuppah and talks to them about how they should love and take care of each other. She also says some blessings and gives them wine to drink.

At my cousin
Marcia's wedding, I
carried a basket of
pink and white
flowers.

Ima writes a lot. She writes letters and speeches and sermons. She also talks on the telephone—too much. People call her to ask questions and invite her to meetings. Sometimes I hear her say, "No. I'm sorry I can't come. Rebecca (that's me!) and I are busy that day." That makes me smile.

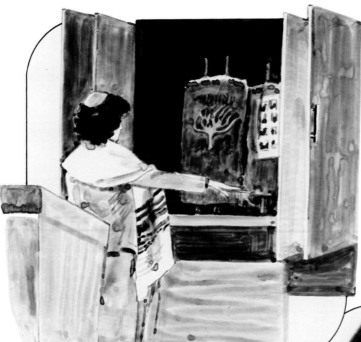

On Friday nights, Ima leads Shabbat services. She stands in front of the ark on the bima.

After the prayers, Ima gives a sermon. Sometimes she tells stories we read in the Torah, and sometimes she makes up new ones.

Abba (that's my dad) and I sit in the front row.
Everybody listens to Ima when she talks, but once I
saw a man sleeping.

After services, everyone comes up to Ima. They all say, "Shabbat shalom, Rabbi." I say, "Shabbat shalom, Ima," and give her a big kiss.

Sometimes, Ima's job doesn't make sense. Jewish people aren't supposed to work on Shabbat and the Jewish holidays, but rabbis have to.

When Ima isn't working on Friday night, we stay home and have special Shabbat dinner. We light candles, sip wine, and sing songs. We say a blessing before we eat and one after. I think the first one is shorter, because God knows we're hungry.

At the end of Shabbat on Saturday night, Abba lights a big, braided candle, and we say Havdallah. We drink some wine, smell sweet spices, and make shadows with our hands in the candlelight. Then Abba puts out the candle in the wine, and I say, "See you next week, Shabbat."

Sometimes Ima does funny things. Last Purim when Abba and I came to the synagogue, we saw someone with a big hat, a curly moustache, and a silly mask. She came right up and hugged me, and then I knew it was Ima!

On Yom Kippur, Ima and I dress all in white. At the end of services, Ima calls out "tekiah gedolah," and I try to hold my breath for as long as Cantor Cohen blows the shofar.

I love the parade on Simchat Torah. Ima
carries a big Torah, and I carry a small one.
Sometimes we march outside and around the block.

On Sunday mornings, Ima and I go to Religious School together. Ima teaches the big kids in Room 8. My class is down the hall in the kindergarten room.

Once, during an assembly, one of the boys threw a paper airplane at his friend, but it hit Ima instead. Ima didn't get angry. She took a crayon, drew a Jewish star on the tail, and told us it was an El Al plane from Israel. Then she asked the pilot to come see her after class.

Later I asked Ima if a star can be Jewish, is the moon Jewish too? She smiled and told Abba what I said. Sometimes parents forget to answer your questions.

Last week, my babysitter Rachel became a Bat Mitzvah. When she finished reading from the Torah, everyone threw candy at her, to wish her a sweet life.

At the end of services, Ima always invites the children to come to the bima to pick up the candy and join her in singing Adon Olam.

I like to stand next to Ima and pretend I'm a rabbi, too. Ima always winks at me and I wink back—at my Ima on the bima.

ABOUT THE AUTHOR

Rabbi Mindy Avra Portnoy, a graduate of Yale University, was ordained at Hebrew Union College—Jewish Institute of Religion in New York, in 1980. A former director of the B'nai B'rith Hillel Foundation at The American University, she currently teaches, lectures, and officiates at life cycle ceremonies. Rabbi Portnoy lives with her husband, Philip L. Breen, and their children, Ceala Eloise and Barney Samuel, in Washington, D.C.

ABOUT THE ARTIST

Steffi Rubin grew up in the Bronx and went to college in San Francisco. She has designed album and book covers, and most recently illustrated *Between the Shadows* by Herman Taube. Her watercolors have won awards from several Maryland art leagues. She paints and draws in Gaithersburg, MD, where she lives with her husband Barry and their two daughters, Shira and Rebecca. Rebecca served as a model for this book.

GLOSSARY

Abba	Daddy
Adon Olam	"Lord of the Universe"—closing hymn
Bat Mitzvah	Attainment of age of religious responsibility
Bima	(Bee-ma) Pulpit
Challah	Sabbath bread
Chuppah	Marriage canopy
El Al	Israel's national airline
Havdallah	Ceremony concluding the Sabbath
Ima	(Ee-ma) Mommy
Kippah	Skullcap
Purim	Joyous holiday celebrating victory against plot to kill the Jews
Shabbat	Sabbath
Shabbat shalom	"A peaceful Sabbath" (Traditional Sabbath greeting)
Shofar	Ram's horn blown on Jewish High Holy Days
Simchat Torah	Holiday celebrating ending and beginning of cycle of reading the Torah
Tallit	Prayer shawl
Tekiah gedolah	Final and longest blast of the shofar
Torah	Five books of Moses
Yom Kippur	Day of Atonement